Close to You

❧ How Animals Bond ❧

Kimiko Kajikawa

Henry Holt and Company ❧ New York

Polar Bears

cuddle in a den of snow.

Ducklings

line up in a single row.

Kangaroos

nestle and go for a ride.

Elephants

walk closely side by side.

Giraffes

pucker up, sniff, and lick.

Dolphins

whistle, clack, and click.

Alligators

lounge in a toothy grin.

Manatees

caress against wrinkly skin.

Porcupines

brush with a prickly nose.

Emperor Penguins

balance on toes.

Snow Monkeys

stare at a friendly face.

Prairie Dogs

snuggle in a warm embrace.

Some people kiss.

Some rub noses.

Some give hugs.

And some give roses.

Everyone cares
in a special way.
How will you care
for someone today?

Polar bears cuddle in a den of snow.

A mother polar bear digs a hole in the snow to prepare to give birth to her cubs. The packed snow makes the inside of the den up to 40 degrees (Fahrenheit) warmer than the outside. When the cubs are born in the winter, they are hairy, blind, deaf, and as small as a rat. By spring, they weigh about 25 pounds and follow their mother, learning how to hunt and swim. Polar bears are found throughout the Arctic. They are in danger because of the warming of their habitat.

Ducklings line up in a single row.

After ducklings hatch, they follow their mother everywhere, often marching single file. To keep them warm and safe from predators, a mother duck may give her ducklings piggyback rides or tuck them under a wing. Ducks are found worldwide except in Antarctica. There are many species of duck. Some species, such as the Hawaiian duck and Laysan duck, are endangered.

Kangaroos nestle and go for a ride.

A newborn kangaroo, called a joey, is bald, blind, and the size of a bean. It spends seven months inside its mother's pouch. By nine months, it prefers to stay outside but returns often to sleep, hide, or drink milk. A joey dives headfirst into the pouch and then does a full somersault to bring its head to the opening. From there, it eats tall grass right from its mother's pouch! Kangaroos are found in Australia and New Guinea. There are many different species of kangaroo. Some species, such as Scott's tree-kangaroo, Goodfellow's tree-kangaroo, and Matschie's tree-kangaroo, are endangered.

Elephants walk closely side by side.

A few hours after birth, an elephant calf is able to walk and follow its mother. The mother elephant never lets her calf out of her sight for the first six months. Elephants are very sensitive to touch. A mother and calf stroke each other with their trunks. Elephants "hug" by wrapping their trunks together in displays of greeting and affection. A young female usually stays with her herd after she is grown (males go off on their own when they are adolescents). Female "babysitters" take care of other elephants' calves as if they were their own. The Asian elephant is endangered; the African elephant is threatened.

Giraffes pucker up, sniff, and lick.

The twelve-foot-tall mother giraffe gives birth standing up. Even though it is a long drop, the calf doesn't get hurt. Instead, the fall helps it take its first big breath. Since giraffes use their sense of smell to recognize one another, mother giraffe often sniffs and noses her calf. She uses her long 18-inch tongue to give her calf a good licking. Giraffes are found in Africa.

Dolphins whistle, clack, and click.

A dolphin is born in the water. Sometimes a newborn dolphin calf is too weak, so the mother guides it to the surface for its first breath of air. Mother and calf whistle, clack, and click at each other. Scientists think that slow clicks and high-pitched whistles are signs of happiness. Every dolphin has its own unique whistle to identify itself. If a calf strays too far, the mother whistles for its return. Calf and mother stay together for the first few months and remain close for many years. Dolphins up to six years old are known to look for their mothers when scared or tired. Dolphins are found in every ocean throughout the world. The Indus River dolphin is endangered.

Alligators lounge in a toothy grin.

A mother alligator makes a large nest and lays 10 to 60 eggs. She keeps guard, leaving only to find nearby shade or to cool off in the water. Just before hatching, the baby alligators call for her with high-pitched squeals. The mother takes the eggs into her mouth and rolls them with her tongue to help the babies hatch. Then, she gently carries the babies to water. Already they can swim and find food, but their mother protects them for three months. She also lets her babies rest in her mouth and on her back. Alligators are found in the southern United States and eastern China. The Chinese alligator is endangered; the American alligator is threatened.

Manatees caress against wrinkly skin.

Manatees are gentle giants. Their skin is thick and wrinkled yet very sensitive to touch. A calf likes to press its face against its mother's skin for reassurance. Manatees love to rub and bump against each other, kiss, embrace with their flippers, and climb on each other's backs. The baby spends close to two years with its mother, learning where to eat and rest. Manatees are found in rivers and along the coasts of West Africa, Amazonia, Central America, and the southeastern United States. The Amazonian and West Indian manatees are endangered species; the West African manatee is threatened.

Porcupines brush with a prickly nose.

A newborn porcupine is born covered with long black hair and with its eyes open. Its quills are soft at birth but harden in less than an hour. The mother porcupine grunts as she noses her baby. Within 15 minutes of birth, the baby will twirl around and wave its tail in the direction of anything unusual. In just a few days, it climbs trees, but it will stay close to its mother for five months. Porcupines are found in Africa, Asia, Central America, North America, and South America. There are about two dozen species of porcupine; the thin-spined porcupine is endangered.

Emperor penguins balance on toes.

After laying an egg, the female emperor penguin gives it to her mate and leaves for the sea to feed. For the next two months, the male balances the egg on his feet and blankets it with his warm belly. He doesn't move because one minute of separation in the Arctic winter will allow the egg to freeze. Temperatures there fall as far as 95 degrees below zero (Fahrenheit). When the female returns with food for the baby chick, it is the male's turn to leave and feed. After that, both parents spend seven weeks sharing the task of caring for the chick. Emperor penguins are found in Antarctica.

Snow monkeys stare at a friendly face.

As soon as it is born, the baby snow monkey (also called a Japanese macaque) and its mother spend countless hours staring at each other's faces. This helps them form a lifetime bond. Male snow monkeys share the parenting duties with the female. The father grooms and carries the baby. The baby nurses for two years and enjoys riding on its mother's back or clinging to her belly and pressing its face against her chest. Snow monkeys are native to Japan. They are a threatened species.

Prairie dogs snuggle in a warm embrace.

Whenever two prairie dogs from the same clan meet, they turn their heads toward each other, open their mouths, and kiss. After the kiss, prairie dogs may groom each other or wrestle. Prairie dogs have between two and eight pups, who chase their parents around in hopes of getting groomed. Fortunately, all prairie dogs from the same clan are more than happy to kiss and groom the pups. Prairie dogs are found in Mexico and the United States. The Mexican prairie dog is an endangered species; the Utah prairie dog is threatened.

Threatened species — likely to become an endangered species.   Endangered species — in danger of extinction.

Some people kiss.

People kiss to show affection. In Belgium, friends greet each other with one kiss on the cheek. In Spain, friends kiss each other twice, once on each check while the Dutch greet each other with three kisses.

Some give hugs.

Many people enjoy giving hugs because they can use their entire body to show they care. Hugs not only feel good but are good for you. Studies have shown that hugs reduce blood pressure, helping to keep the heart healthy.

Some rub noses.

Some anthropologists think that touching lips happened naturally when people rubbed noses. The Inuit people rub noses to nuzzle and show affection.

And some give roses.

In many parts of the world, people give roses to show love, affection, and friendship. Rose colors have special meanings. Red roses mean love. Yellow roses mean friendship and joy. Dark pink roses mean thank you.

Everyone cares in a special way.
How will you care for someone today?

- What do your parents do that make you feel cared for?

- How do other people make you feel safe and secure?

- How do you show your parents that you care?

- How do you show other people that you care?

- Do you have any pets? How do you care for them? How do they care for you?

Birth to Adulthood

	Number of babies	Weight at birth	Weight at maturity	Age of independence
Polar Bear	1–3	1–1½ lbs.	400–1,500 lbs.	2 yrs.
Duck (mallard)	5–14	1 oz.	2 lbs.	8 wks.
Kangaroo (red)	1	less than ⅟₃₀ oz.	50–200 lbs.	18 mos.
Elephant	1	110–265 lbs.	6,000–15,000 lbs.	3–10 yrs.
Giraffe	1	100–225 lbs.	1,000–4,000 lbs.	1 yr.
Dolphin (bottlenose)	1	44 lbs.	300–1,400 lbs.	3–6 yrs.
Alligator	10–60	2 oz.	400–1,000 lbs.	2 yrs.
Manatee	1	65 lbs.	400–1,300 lbs.	2 yrs.
Porcupine (tree)	1	1 lb.	2–20 lbs.	5 mos.
Emperor Penguin	1	1 oz.	60–90 lbs.	13 mos.
Snow Monkey	1	1 lb.	20–40 lbs.	3 yrs.
Prairie Dog	2–8	½ oz.	2–4 lbs.	1 yr.
Human	1–2	3–12 lbs.	80–250 lbs.	18 yrs.

(Numbers in table are approximate normal ranges per gestation.)

Animal Web Sites of Interest

- Animal Diversity Web: http://animaldiversity.ummz.umich.edu
- BBC Science and Nature: www.bbc.co.uk/nature/animals
- Electronic Zoo: http://netvet.wustl.edu/ssi.htm
- San Diego Zoo: www.sandiegozoo.org/animalbytes
- Sea World: www.seaworld.org/animal-info

To Ted-san with love and hugs

ACKNOWLEDGMENTS

Academy of Natural Sciences, Conservation International, Walter Hintz,
Jeff Munson, Christy Ottaviano, Keiko Saito, San Diego Zoo, David Stringer,
Wildlife Conservation Society, Jonathan Wright

Permission for use of the following photographs is gratefully acknowledged:

Polar bears (cover): © Kennan Ward/Corbis; emperor penguins (front jacket flap and interior): Nature Picture Library,
photo by David Tipling; prairie dogs (title page and interior): Gayle Harper; polar bears: Ginger Gunn/Barber Nature Photography;
ducks: AP/Wide World Photos; kangaroos: Photographers Direct, photo by Sue and Stan Russell; elephants: Eagle Visions Photography,
photo by Craig Lovell; giraffes: AP/Wide World Photos; dolphins: Frans Lanting; alligators: Cactus Clyde Productions, photo by C. C.
Lockwood; manatees: Nature Picture Library, photo by Jyrgen Freund; porcupines: Tom & Pat Leeson Photography; snow monkeys:
Kazuyuki Saito; mother and daughter kissing: Brand X/Jupiter Images; father and daughter rubbing noses: Jim and Mary
Whitmer; father and son hugging: Banana Stock/Jupiter Images; boy with roses: Banana Stock/Jupiter Images.

Henry Holt and Company, LLC
Publishers since 1866
175 Fifth Avenue
New York, New York 10010
www.HenryHoltKids.com

Henry Holt® is a registered trademark of Henry Holt and Company, LLC.
Copyright © 2008 by Kimiko Kajikawa
All rights reserved. Distributed in Canada by H. B. Fenn and Company Ltd.

Library of Congress Cataloging-in-Publication Data
Kajikawa, Kimiko.
Close to you : how animals bond / Kimiko Kajikawa.
p.   cm.
ISBN-13: 978-0-8050-8123-7 / ISBN-10: 0-8050-8123-2
1. Animals—Infancy—Juvenile literature.
2. Parental behavior in animals—Juvenile literature. I. Title.
QL763.K35 2008   591.3'9—dc22   2007002959

First Edition—2008 / Designed by Véronique Lefèvre Sweet
Printed in China on acid-free paper. ∞
3 5 7 9 10 8 6 4 2